EARLY LEARNING WITH LETTS
three- to five-year-olds

Pirates in the Park

Story by Pie Corbett
Activities by David Bell, Pie Corbett,
Geoff Leyland and Mick Seller

Illustrations by Diann Timms

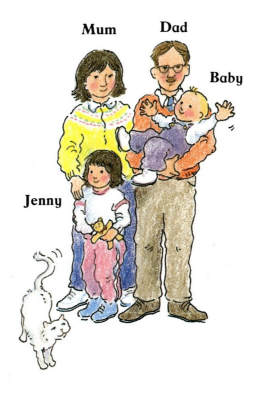

For Edward

Jenny and Baby were waiting for Dad.
'Quick, Dad's coming.'

Who is coming up the path?
Where is he coming from?

Do you think he's bringing something with him?

What will Jenny and Baby do when he comes in?

'What did you two do today?'

What shapes can you see here?
How many circles can you see?
How many squares can you see?
Point to the shapes that have three sides.
Point to the shapes that have four sides.

... saw a kite fly...

Can you see the kite in the picture?
How do you think it stays up in the sky?
Do you think it is a windy day?
Can you see anything else moving in the wind in the picture?
Can you think of things which the wind moves which are not in the picture?

How many balls can you see?
Look for a group of three children.
Count the children to make sure.
Are there two groups of four pirates
or three groups of four pirates?
Count them together.
If one of the pirates on deck chairs
went back to the ship, how many would be left?

Which balloon is a different shape from the rest? Why is it different?

Are all the other balloons exactly the same? Point to the ones that are bigger.

How many different colours are the balloons?

Can you find a big red balloon? Can you see a small green one?

When you next go to feed the ducks, look at them carefully.

Do different ducks eat in different ways?

Do they all like bread?

How do they eat it? Have they got teeth?

Listen to the different sounds the ducks make. What do you think they mean?

WATCH OUT Don't go too near the water. Ducks can feel grumpy so don't let them take the bread out of your hand – you might be pecked!

You could try out some boats at bath-time. Collect four or five plastic lids, margarine containers or things like that.

Load each one with building blocks until it sinks. Count the blocks. Which boat could carry the most blocks? Can you see why?

Do you know any stories about boats and water?

What is happening in this picture?
What are the pirates doing?
What are they using to help them climb?
Do you think they will fall?

Can you see Jenny? Who is pushing her?
Do you like swinging high?
What do you like to do when you go to the park?

. . . looked at the flowers. . .

Try looking really closely at flowers.
When you're next outside, choose two or
three flowers to look at.

What colour are they?

Do they smell?

Are the flowers big or small? What shape are they?

What sort of leaves do they have?

What is inside the flower?

Do you ever keep your Mum waiting?

Can you think of some funny excuses?

Maybe an elephant stopped you . . . Maybe. . .

Point to all the animals in the picture.

Point to all the boys.

Point to all the girls.

Now point to all the pirates.

Who is wearing blue?

Who has dark hair?

How many furry animals can you see?

Can you think of another way to sort the animals?

Can you tell different kinds of food by their smell?

Choose six foods. Put a little of each on plates and cover them with tissues. Take it in turns to smell the food and guess what each one is. What words can you use – strong, sweet, spicy, sour? Now taste each food (try not to peep!) Do you think you are right? Take the tissues away and look together.

The ice-creams the children are eating are many different colours.
Can you name the colours?

Look at the colours.
Are they the same in each ice-cream?
How are they different?
What order would you put the colours in?

Can you see any other patterns in the picture?

Not much happened really.'

Activity notes

Pages 2–3 Part of learning to read is making sensible guesses about what might come next. These sorts of questions help your child to talk about what is going on in the story. In this way you can build up the story together.

Pages 4–5 When we choose a book to read most of us rely on the cover to tell us what it is about. Children need to get used to looking at covers for clues about the kind of book they are holding.

Pages 6–7 Exploring shapes is something children do at a very early age. You can help them to practise shape words such as 'circles', 'squares', 'triangles' by looking at toys, games and household objects. This will lead children to discover for themselves the different characteristics of shapes, eg the number of sides they have.

Page 8–9 Encourage an awareness of the wind and its effects by looking at what happens on windy days to trees, clouds, washing, etc, and talking about it together.
Flying a simple kite is a most enjoyable way to find out what the wind does.

Pages 10–11 As children become more proficient in counting, they will begin to see groups of objects in two, threes, fours. You could encourage your child to group objects such as toy bricks or cars in this way. They can then go on to count the number of groups.

Pages 12–13 Identifying the odd one out helps children to see in which way objects are the same or different. Children will find their own ways of identifying objects, according to size, colour, texture, etc. This will lead to more accurate definitions, for example, 'all the balloons are red, but they are different sizes'.

Pages 14–15 This activity encourages careful observation and helps to develop children's understanding of living things: their different diets and feeding habits.
You could follow this up by looking at different types of birds feeding in your garden or in the park: do they eat berries, seeds, worms?

Pages 16–17 Many young children think that small things float and big things sink. This bath-time experiment will help them to understand the principles of floating and sinking.
You could follow this up by testing several different objects in a bowl of water. Your child could choose the objects and predict which will sink, and which will float.

Pages 18–19 One way of bringing a story alive is through questions which invite children to talk about their own lives. The questions will help your child to make real links and feel what the characters are feeling. It helps to question and then listen.
You can also talk about a time when you both did something together.

Pages 20–21 Young children are often fascinated to see how things grow and develop. Ask them if they know where flowers come from. Look for flowering plants alongside seed pods and seedlings: talk about the sorts of plants you could grow from a dandelion seed, acorn, etc.

Pages 22–23 Thinking up funny ideas develops a child's sense of invention. It also makes story reading fun, and if it is fun children will want to return to it again and again. It is worth encouraging this, as learning about books needs practice.

Pages 24–25 In this activity the children are grouping the people and animals into sets. This is a central skill in early maths.
Encourage your child to find as many different sets as possible from the picture. Doing this will help to enhance logical thinking.

Pages 26–27 This helps children to think carefully about the smell and taste of everyday foods, and also to use language accurately in defining the different smells and tastes.
Using only one sense at a time, without looking at the food, is quite difficult. Usually we rely on a combination of the senses.

Pages 28–29 Becoming aware of patterns in shapes and colours is an important first step in maths. It helps to develop a visual understanding of order.
Children enjoy threading different coloured beads. Suggest they experiment with putting them in as many different orders as they like.

Pages 30–31 You could follow up this story by drawing some pirates and giving them names. You could make up a pirate story together. A good starting point for stories is 'What would happen if . . .?'